RAILWAY
SERIES

THE PAIGNTON & DARTMOUTH RAILWAY

MIKE HEATH

HALSGROVE

First published in Great Britain in 2008

British Library Cataloguing-in-Publication Data
A CIP record for this title is available from the British Library

ISBN 978 1 84114 741 3

HALSGROVE
Halsgrove House
Ryelands Industrial Estate
Bagley Road, Wellington, Somerset TA21 9PZ
Tel: 01823 653777   Fax: 01823 216796
email: sales@halsgrove.com
website: www.halsgrove.com

Printed and bound by
Grafiche Flaminia, Italy

INTRODUCTION

In the early nineteenth century the steep hillsides around the estuary of the River Dart, in South Devon, greatly impaired the transportation of goods to and from the riverside town of Dartmouth. At that time horses laden with pannier baskets provided the only overland transport and whilst the development of turnpike roads with gradients that gave access to horse drawn carriages and carts improved the situation the transport of goods was still seriously restricted. The need for a rail connection was clearly evident.

The first railway in the area was opened by the South Devon Railway between Exeter and Plymouth. The first section, connecting Exeter with Newton Abbot was opened in 1846 and extended to Totnes the following year. That same year saw completion of a branch line to Torquay. Set up by local gentlemen, The Dartmouth and Torbay Railway Company then sought to extend this branch to Dartmouth. As ever the work was carried out and opened in stages. Paignton was reached in 1859, Churston in 1861 with the final section to Kingswear following in 1864. Attempts, in 1860, to introduce a deviation taking the line to Dittisham Ferry with a view to bridging the Dart at a later date were foiled following objections from an obviously influential local landowner leaving Dartmouth a ferry ride away from the Kingswear terminus. Nevertheless a station was provided with full booking and parcels facilities and Dartmouth became unique in possessing a railway station that has never seen a train!

By the 1890s the Newton Abbot to Kingswear branch had generated a substantial volume of traffic contributing considerably to the growth of the Torbay area as a major holiday resort, a situation that continued well into the 1950s. There was also substantial freight traffic with the demands of Torquay Gas Works requiring a steady flow of coal traffic from the quayside at Kingswear in addition to the general freight merchandise conveyed to local businesses.

At the end of the sixties the Paignton to Kingswear branch was threatened with closure by British Rail but the Dart Valley Railway Company, who had already taken over the running of the Totnes to Buckfastleigh branch some years earlier, grasped the opportunity to acquire this section of line and almost without break commenced train services under their own banner in 1973. Ownership of the Buckfastleigh branch has since passed to the South Devon Railway Preservation Society, allowing the Dart Valley Railway PLC to acquire boat and bus companies to provide a 'seamless transport of delight through one of the most beautiful areas of England'.

The train journey travels through superb scenery. Starting in the traditional seaside town of Paignton this holiday line then follows the spectacular Torbay coast along the cliffs overlooking the bay before turning inland towards Churston. There then follows a couple of miles of pastoral Devon before the line passes through the wooded slopes of the Dart Valley descending to sea level along the river bank on the final approach to Kingswear. This final stretch is arguably the loveliest section of railway in the country with the vista of the Dart estuary and its fascinating variety of boats and yachts with the 'olde-world' town of Dartmouth and world famous Britannia Naval College on the opposite bank.

This is my family's favourite area in the country; I hope this album conveys the reasons why!

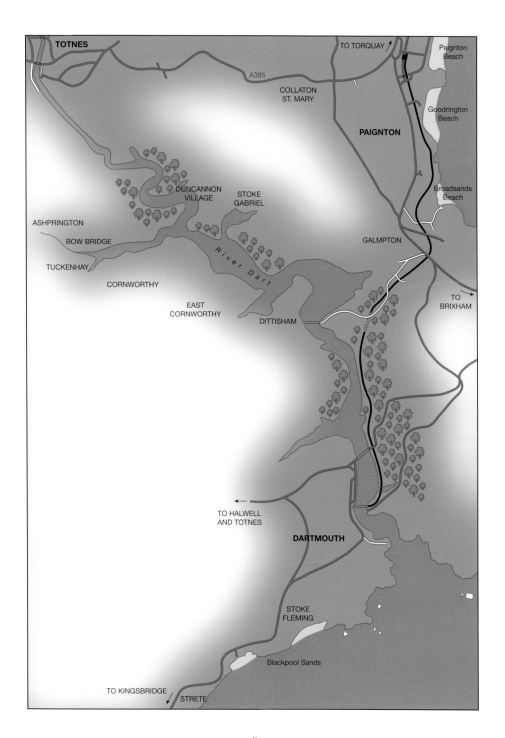

Paignton Station is situated in the town centre alongside the Network Rail station and whilst it is not the most impressive introduction to a railway and a total contrast to the scenery through which the line passes, it does do exactly what it says on the awning. And the sight and sound of a steam locomotive simmering alongside the platform will always attract the attention of holiday-makers.

At the end of 2007 the railway's 'home' fleet consisted of six steam locomotives. The most recent arrival is former British Railway's Class 4MT 4-6-0 No. 75014 which was built in Swindon in 1951 and worked extensively across the national network until withdrawal. In preservation it has visited many heritage railways and worked numerous main-line specials including the 'Jacobite' trains between Fort William and Mallaig in the west of Scotland which is when it received the name 'Braveheart'. It was purchased by the Dart Valley Railway in 2003.

The 4500 Class 2-6-2 tank locomotives were introduced in 1906 for use on the many Great Western Railway branch lines. No. 4555 spent much of its working life on such lines in Devon and Cornwall. It was purchased straight out of service, in 1965, by the then Dart Valley Railway. It now carries the name 'Warrior'.

Former Great Western Railway
2-6-2 tank No. 4588 is a Class 4575,
built in 1927, but basically the same
design as No 4555. The most notable
difference is the larger side tanks
which have a distinctive slope along
their forward top edge. This
locomotive was saved from the cutter's
torch being rescued from the Barry
Island scrapyard in 1971. The Dart
Valley Railway Association bought it for
the princely sum of £1750! Its
preservation name is 'Trojan'.

Built for heavy freight work 5205 Class 2-8-0 tank No. 5239 spent its entire working life hauling coal trains in the Welsh Valleys. It was built at Swindon in 1924, withdrawn by British Railways in 1963 and subsequently purchased for preservation from the scrap yard in Barry Island in 1973. Initial restoration was extensive and it wasn't until 1978 that it entered service on the preserved line. This is the most powerful preserved tank engine type in Britain and the very appropriate name 'Goliath' was bestowed on it in 1978.

0-6-0 Pannier Tanks were the jack of all trades on the Great Western Railway carrying out many important duties such as local branch line passenger and freight services, station pilot duties and general shunting operations. Of the many types constructed, the Paignton and Dartmouth Railway has one example. No. 6435 represents the 6400 Class, a variant that had larger wheels more suitable for light passenger duties. It was built in 1937 and purchased straight from British Rail in 1965. Named 'Ajax' it is used to haul the lighter trains on the line.

The 'Manor' Class was born out of the need for a lightweight passenger locomotive to replace ageing tank engines on the lightly laid lines in mid-Wales. No. 7827 'Lydham Manor', which dates from 1950, spent all its life in Wales and saw occasional use on Royal Trains. In 1965 it was withdrawn and sent to Barry scrapyard from where it was rescued four years later and re-entered traffic in 1972.

Prior to the start of the 2008 services news emerged that the railway had bolstered its fleet by the purchase of former Great Western Railway 42000 Class 2-8-0 tank No. 4277. Like 'Goliath' this freight engine spent much of its working life in South Wales hauling heavy freight including coal, steel and iron ore on the steeply graded valley lines. In preservation it has visited many heritage railways including Llangollen where it carried a British Railways black livery.

No. 4555 and 'Lydham Manor' attract attention at the Kingswear end of the platform.
This photograph dates from what was probably my first visit to the area in August 1976.

Opposite: Here in a Great Western livery No. 4277 stands alongside the coaling stage at the
Didcot Railway Centre near Oxford during one their anuual photography evenings.

Prior to each departure the locomotive will take water from the column on the run-round loop and early arrivals for the first train of the day may also witness the coal conveyor in operation as the tender or tank engine's bunker are filled with the day's fuel.

Most of the platform is under cover which is ideal for providing protection against the extremes of our summer rain and occasional sunshine, but with a line of trees shading the boundary with the adjacent playing fields the dimly lit station is not the most conducive for photography. However the use of shadows, light and a porter with a trolley can give pleasing results.

At departure time the guard will blow his whistle and with the wave of his green flag the train will ease out of the station – however not before the fireman has operated a plunger that starts the level crossing closure procedure, to stop vehicles passing across Sands Road Crossing which is just outside the station limits.

Now the cylinder drain cocks have been closed
the locomotive is revealed as Great Western
Manor class 4-6-0 No. 7827 'Lydham Manor'
which was actually built by British Rail in 1950,
two years after the GWR had ceased to be. Once
over the crossing the beat of the steam gains
momentum as the train accelerates on its way.

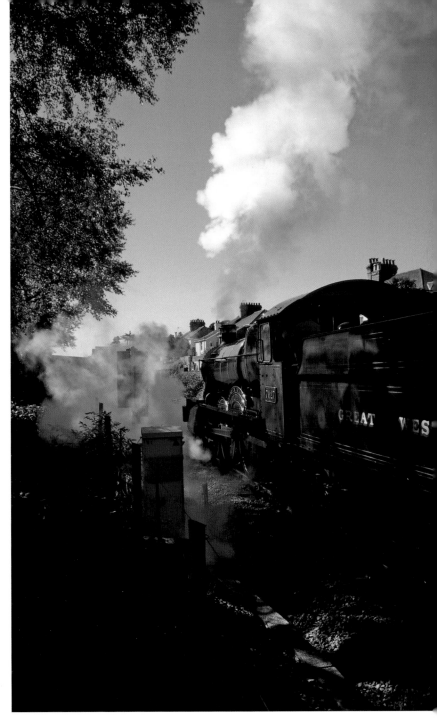

The first three-quarters of a mile is parallel to Network Rail's carriage sidings and runs through the southern residential area of Paignton before opening out on the approach to Goodrington Sands alongside Young's Park. The collection of beach huts huddled on the car park alongside the track indicates that the main holiday season is over.

For the high season the huts are released from their winter hibernation and stand proudly on the promenade alongside Goodrington Sands. As this first train of the day pulled out of the station there was only one family on the beach to acknowledge it, and one photographer up to his knees in water! Twisting their way through the air in the background are the gigantic flumes of the Quaywest water park.

A passenger's view of the beach as yet another pedestrian partakes
in the time-honoured tradition of waving to a passing train.

British summers don't always play by the rules. The hefty cloaking on the beachcombers suggests that the temperature is somewhat disappointing, but the heavy sky does give the scene an atmospheric backdrop.

The headland at the northern end of the bay is dominated by the red rocks of Roundham Head.
The cliffs are set out as gardens with a network of paths . . .

Opposite:
. . . from where there are superb views of the sands and the railway.

Right from the platform end of Goodrington Station the line climbs steeply.
The severity of the gradient is evident as 'Warrior' passes over the beach end of Cliff Park Road.

The sea was still lapping around my knees and my rolled up jeans were beginning to
soak up water as I turned to get the going-away shot of the train seen earlier on page 21.

Leaving the golden sands of Goodrington behind, the beach soon gives way to rocky cliffs and small coves. Another view from the train with the sun just out of shot to the left providing dramatic backlighting to a stunning cloud formation.

Opposite:
Readers of any of my earlier Railway Series books for Halsgrove will be aware that I usually include photographs taken by younger son Karl. Here for the first time is one taken by my wife! Whilst I remained nearer sea level she had wandered along the cliff paths above Roundham Head and captured the steam trail of the train perfectly. (I didn't tell her that at the time though.) (Photo Shirley Heath)

As the train plays hide and seek along the cliff top the first small inlet, Saltern Cove, comes into view.

The coastal footpath along this stretch provides many vantage points from where you can watch, and photograph, the trains as they pass by. The grassy mound rising to the left of the track beyond the Waterside holiday park is Sugar Loaf Hill and on a clear day wonderful panoramic views across the whole bay can be had from here.

It is also a great place to capture a side on-view of the train as it continues the climb above Saltern Cove.

Opposite:
You can spend all day at Waterside as there are many photographic vantage points.
Morning trains are best captured from the seaward side of the track.

As the train passes the Cove passengers are treated to a vista that covers a vast area.
In the middle distance is Brixham with Berry Head on the extreme left.

On this stretch of the line the outlook is spectacular whichever way you face.

Once past the holiday park the line rises sharply again and travels through a section cut through cliffs.

Opposite:
No, the area has not been overrun by genetically modified giant moles. Recent trackside clearance has enabled ramblers on the coastal path to observe almost the entire length of the train.

As the journey continues it is not long before the next break in the
cliff face reveals the extent of Broadsands Beach . . .

Opposite:
. . . and from the beach a first glimpse of the steam train

At this point the railway begins to turn away from the coast and crosses over Broadsands Viaduct seen here from the main A379 Paignton to Brixham road. The substantial breakwater at Brixham draws attention in the background.

Opposite:
The charming tranquillity of an out of season Broadsands Beach is barely disturbed by the passing train.

Broadsands Viaduct which is the first of three such structures on the railway is 51yards long,
75 feet high and has 4 arches. (It was built well before metrication!)

Opposite:
After passing through a deep cutting the train again comes within sight of the
beach as it emerges on the even longer Hookhills Viaduct.

Opposite and above:
Hookhills Viaduct has 9 arches, is 116 yards long and stands 85 feet above a residential estate
which has developed in the valley below and leads down to Broadsands Beach.

For a small supplementary charge passengers can travel in the 'Devon Belle' observation car.
If evidence was needed of the spectacular seascape visible from this coach then this photograph provides it.

Opposite:
Inland on Bascombe Road, located just off the main Dartmouth Road, there is a
welcoming park bench which overlooks the viaduct and bay beyond. 'Warrior' is about to disappear
into another cutting and veer away inland towards the line's summit at Churston.

In its former life Churston Station was also a terminus for the branch line to Brixham, closed in 1963. The second track, which forms a passing loop allowing two train operation in high season was restored in the late seventies. The station is looked after by a small group of volunteers.

On a gloriously sunny day in September 2004, 'Braveheart' glides into the station.

With only a single train operating on that day it was not long before the train was on its way to Kingswear.

Opposite:
From Churston the rest of the journey to Kingswear is virtually all downhill and at first is through deeply rolling countryside. 'Lydham Manor' is about to enter the 495-yard long Greenway Tunnel.

On exiting the tunnel the train emerges into a stunning change of scenery, high above the wooded slopes bordering the Dart Estuary. One of the first clear views of the river is across the creeks from behind the old shipyard, now sadly defunct, of Philip & Son. Until 1923 the railway passed above the entrance to Noss and Longwood Creek (pictured here) on two wooden viaducts. As the yard became busier and the vessels bigger the viaducts were proving to be a major obstacle. So a 'deviation' of the line was engineered to take it round a curve behind the yard.

Boat building started back in 1891 by the partnership Simpson Strickland and their then state-of-the-art yard built steam yachts in timber and steel and lead. Whilst the First World War brought much work in, it also brought bankruptcy to the partners who, in 1918, sold the concern to Philip & Son. Under their ownership the works became a major shipbuilding centre for the South West. Work included building hundreds of vessels for the Admiralty and many lightships for Trinity House. More than 500 workers were employed during the Second World War and the yard continued to provide employment until the 1960s when it was sold to a Totnes-based timber merchants. Today all shipbuilding and repair work has ceased and its current status is that of a marina.

It's not long before the line emerges from the riverside woods.

At this point the train is slowing on the approach to Britannia Crossing . . .

. . . and passengers get first sight of their destination, Dartmouth, and its ever expanding harbour with crafts of all sizes moored as far as the eye can see.

The level crossing carries the main road from Torbay to Dartmouth via the Higher Ferry which leaves from the adjacent slipway. To be strictly accurate as the 'ferry' is permanently attached to both banks by steel cables, which guide the vessel across the river, it is actually designated a 'floating bridge'. The original 1831 model was steam powered but this proved to be too expensive and was replaced by two horses working a treadmill. This two horsepower system continued until 1867 when Philip & Son took the operation over reintroducing steam. The present diesel powered ferry was introduced in 1960.

For the remaining three-quarters of a mile from Britannia Crossing all the way to Kingswear the railway runs along the water's edge . . .
(Photo Karl Heath)

Opposite:
. . . separated only by a narrow footpath which provides a number of vantage points for photography.

Complementing the already magnificent river scenery of the Dart Valley are the dense oak woods that cloak the hillside. Hoodown Wood provides the backdrop as 'Braveheart' descends towards the terminus.

A popular Dart Valley Trail walk crosses the line a few hundred yards from the station necessitating a warning blast on the whistle from approaching locomotives.

'Lydham Manor' crosses Waterhead Viaduct within sight of the station platforms.

The restrictive headroom of the viaduct limits the size of crafts that can pass beneath. (Photo Karl Heath)

Thus, Waterhead Creek remains a tranquil haven providing sheltered anchorage and a stark contrast with . . .

. . . the affluence on show on the other side of the bridge!

Film buffs might recognise Kingswear Station, as the railway scenes in the film
'The French Lieutenant's Woman' were shot here. Behind the sloping parapet on the left is Fore Street …

… a vantage point from where you can take in the breathtaking panorama over the water…

… and follow the progress of the next train as it snakes its way along the river bank.

The train journey is almost complete but the destination is still a ferry trip away.

Alongside the railway terminus is the Royal Dart Hotel built to provide accommodation for rail passengers awaiting the arrival of their ships for onward journeys across the sea. To the left of the hotel is the path from the station down to the passenger ferry pontoon, to the right is the Lower Ferry slipway. Fortuitously both ferries are in attendance.

Opposite:
The overall roof at the buffer stop end of the station is a listed structure, being one of the only two surviving examples of a once-common Isambard Kingdom Brunel design still in railway use.

This rare example of a covered country terminus has been superbly restored and is sometimes used to protect some of the railway's stock from inclement weather.

On this occasion an empty shed reveals the intricate detail of the structure. 'Warrior' completes a scene that but for the preservation era nameplate could date from many decades ago. (Photo Karl Heath)

The external elevation of the station building is little changed. The Great Western Railway notice boards which would once have been covered with various railway timetables now provide information for today's tourists.

From 1999 the Dart Valley Railway Plc has owned and operated, under the trading
name of River Link, a fleet of ferries and cruise vessels providing a variety of excursions on the river.
One of the passenger ferries arrives at the Kingswear pontoon.

The Lower 'Car' Ferry arrives at the Dartmouth slipway as the River Link's flagsip, the *Dart Explorer*
returns from the harbour mouth where its passengers will have been treated to the open sea view of the Castle.

This particular Tudor castle was built between 1481 and 1491 and at the time provided a state-of-the-art defence, being one of the first to be purpose-built to house cannon. There was a second castle with cannon built on the Kingswear side. Woe betide any shipping that considered running the gauntlet of the crossfire between these two castles! Prominent above the castle is the church of S. Petrock and the cream-coloured tower standing proud on the headland was originally a lighthouse built in 1856.

Today the castle is managed by English Heritage and is well worth a visit.

A river cruise is another must for the visitor if only to listen to the entertaining commentary of the skipper.

Bayards Cove is perhaps the most recognisable section of the waterfront due to its association with the popular television drama 'The Onedin Line'. The old quay, once known as Bears Cove, has as its centrepiece the eighteenth century Customs House (on the right in this photograph).

A memorial plaque sited on the quay commemorates the
town's link with the Pilgrim Fathers. In 1620 the
Mayflower and *Speedwell* came into Dartmouth
for repairs to the latter, before continuing their
journey to the New World. (Given the wonderful
setting and the adjacent convivial public house
I would have been tempted to stay here.)

Opposite:
The 'Soap on the Sea' series ran for over 90 episodes
transmitted between 1971 and 1980. In 1976 during
one of my earliest visits the 'Onedin's' ship the
Charlotte Rose was in port!

Dartmouth has long boasted a station with no trains. The 1889 building provided a booking office and full parcels facilities and even despatched motor cars down a covered gangway which ran from under the awning on the right. The building today is little changed but alas is no longer a part of the railway.

Regatta Week includes a gathering
of steam-powered boats.

The 'Boat Float' was an open quayside prior to the construction of the South Embankment in 1885. The Royal Court Hotel started life as two prominent merchants' houses built on the quayside.

Foss Street takes its name from the 'Foss' which was a dam built across a creek to link the two early settlements of Clifton and Hardness that combined have become Dartmouth. The street follows the line of the original embankment.

The Royal Avenue Gardens marks an area of land, aptly called the 'New Ground',
reclaimed from the river in the seventeenth century.

The best vantage point for an aerial view of the area is Jawbones Hill.
The climb through the colourful streets is somewhat strenuous . . .

Opposite:
. . . but the panoramic reward is well worth it giving a bird's eye view of the station
as 'Braveheart' and its train arrive at the Kingswear terminus.

From what must be one of the most idyllically located park benches, the return working can be followed from Kingswear to beyond Britannia Crossing before disappearing from view altogether as it starts to cut its way through the wooded hillside.

Opposite:
The view towards the mouth of the river isn't bad either.

Inland the imposing Britannia Royal Naval College stands majestically
on the hillside overlooking the town and harbour.

Opened in 1905 the college replaced two ships, HMS *Britannia* and HMS *Hindustan* which had been permanently anchored in the harbour since the 1860s. These two relics from the days of Nelson were home and school to over 200 officer-cadets and remained in use for 53 years until the health and safety concerns of the time saw plans for a shore-based facility come to fruition. The reconstructed ship's figurehead from *Britannia* guards the parade ground. Guided tours are advertised at the Dartmouth Tourist Information Centre.

The Dartmouth Heritage Trail is a walk through the medieval streets past many historic buildings with fascinating frontages such as those in Fairfax Place, and calling at the 'Cherub Inn' which having been built around 1380 has the distinction of being the oldest building in the town.

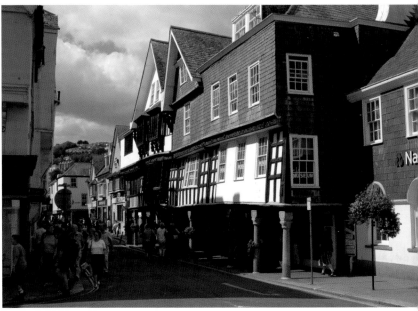

The 'Butterwalk' is a lovely Tudor building which survived unchanged for 300 years before suffering bomb damage in 1943. The building was restored in 1954. At one end, Parade House, was demolished in 1980 and sensitively rebuilt with a slate hung front.

Fireworks apart, evening trains are unusual on this railway but back in July 1988 a locomotive whistle echoing across the water alerted me to some late shunting activities in progress.

So the next available ferry was boarded and a number of photographs taken in the golden light at sunset.

By dusk that same evening a sharp shower had dampened the platform as
'Goliath' awaited the return of its private charter passengers.

Opposite:
The grand finale of Regatta Week is a spectacular firework display. As you can imagine the roads
and car parks are substantially over subscribed at this time so as the old logo used to proclaim it's best
to let the 'train take the strain'. The P&DR runs a special evening service to the event.

The pyrotechnics are launched from floating pontoons in front of the promenade at Dartmouth, but in my opinion are best viewed from the Kingswear side. (Unless of course you own, or know a man that owns, a boat!)

Opposite:
For the duration of the spectacle the town's street lighting is turned off. The pinpricks of light from the buildings and the floodlit Naval College create an eerie backcloth.

Without doubt this must be
one of the best firework displays
in the country. Once over it's a quick
dash back to the station to catch the
special back to Paignton.

Opposite:
The Regatta Fair's 'big wheel' is
dwarfed by the cascading inferno.

Class 25 Diesel No. D7535 is often seen on works trains and on the rare occasion that a steam locomotive fails, railway speak for 'breaks down', it can provide a rescue service. In keeping with the company's naming policy it has been christened 'Hercules'.

The imminent arrival of the service train required D7535 to vacate the main platform. The footbridge in the foreground dates from 1896 and many photographs of the station, including the previous one, are taken from it.

'Ajax' awaits the return of the fireman who has just completed changing the
points to allow the locomotive to run round the train.

Opposite:
No. 75014 'Braveheart' crosses Waterhead Viaduct at low tide.

Kingswear is a popular destination for steam-hauled excursions from all over the country and the locomotives that haul these specials sometimes spend a few weeks on the railway operating the service trains. Former Great Western Railway No 7802 'Bradley Manor' has been a regular visitor from the Severn Valley Railway.

Opposite:
The 'Torbay Express' is one such special which originates in Bristol and arrives in Kingswear around lunchtime. 'Bradley Manor' having just come off its train will reverse all the way back to Churston to be turned on the turntable.

Later in the afternoon having been watered and coaled it has returned to Kingswear to take charge of the return working.

After a pleasant summer's day in Dartmouth, which will no doubt have included a delicious Devon Cream Tea, passengers make their way back to the train.

Meanwhile the locomotive has completed the run round and hooked on to the stock.

No. 4555 is ready for the 'off'.

All aboard for the trip back to Paignton.

Opposite:
Before the train can receive the green light, and start out on the return journey, the barriers
controlling the crossing to the Dart Marina will have to be dropped into place. These are
worked from the signal box at Britannia Crossing under CCTV observation.

Whereas most preserved railways try to retain and restore traditional semaphore signalling the commercially operated P&DR has installed the modern coloured lights all controlled from the one signal box. The signalman can see from a track diagram where each train is at any given moment.

114

The circular construction that affords grandstand views of all railway activities is known locally as the 'Banjo', and is actually a turning circle introduced into the village's road system to improve the flow of traffic. I wonder if it would have been as necessary if the original railway had been retained and improved.

Great Western Railway 'Hall' Class 4-6-0 No.4920 'Dumbleton Hall', which was built in Swindon in 1929, passes over Waterhead Creek in July 1992. The locomotive is based on the South Devon Railway where it is currently awaiting restoration work.

In the golden age of steam the railway would have dominated this scene. On the land to the left of the line there was a signalbox, carriage sidings, locomotive turntable and a cattle dock. More sidings, full of coal trucks, would have occupied the wharf on the river side of the station.

While I was perched on a set of concrete steps composing the rail level shot my younger son, Karl, had ventured into the creek for a totally different perspective. (Photo Karl Heath)

Opposite:
In August 2003 'Bradley Manor' having travelled to Devon at the head of an excursion had been 'failed' on arrival at Kingswear. After repairs were carried out at the railway's works a period of 'running in' followed allowing a pleasantly surprised holidaymaker cum photographer to record this unexpected visit.

The geese and swans were unperturbed by the photographer wading
with them on the shoreline of Waterhead Creek.

Opposite:
On this particular occasion, in July 1992, my elder son, Darren, was alongside me and took a photograph of No. 6435
on the next departure. His effort won him that year's Transport Category in the *Amateur Photographer* magazine's
'Photographer of the Year' competition with the presentation held at BAFTA in London.

Also in service that day was No. 4555 'Warrior'.

On a later occasion I couldn't resist including a touch of colour in the foreground as 'Warrior' headed back to Paignton.

A pristine 'Trojan' pulls away past Hoodown sidings and its collection of permanent way paraphernalia.

A shaft of sunlight picks out the train meandering its way along the edge of the river.

Wall to wall light from an unblinking sun highlights all the detail of this Paignton-bound train.

Contrary to first impressions not all the sailing craft on the river hail from the most recent London Boat Show!

With the footpath and railway hugging the river bank passengers and walkers are treated to superb uninterrupted views of estuary life and activities

The jungle-like woods that create such an impressive backcloth to the river inspired the producer of one series of 'The Onedin Line' to use those upstream of the railway as a cheap substitute for the Amazon rain forest. Rubber alligators moored to rafts looked convincing but the sight of Amazonian Indian smoke signals passing through the wood in one episode took the deception a bit too far. (It was in fact a steam train heading for Churston.)

With the woods in their autumn colours and the Higher Ferry across the river its all aboard for a pleasant
sail on the tranquil waters. Looks like 'Fido' may need some persuading though!

Opposite:
A splendid choice of activity for visitors to enjoy be it a steam-hauled train journey,
a paddle ferry crossing or a relaxing river cruise.

'Goliath' powers away from Britannia Crossing, next stop Churston. (Photo Karl Heath)

Once past the crossing the line climbs sharply and the locomotive will have to work hard
for the next couple of miles with gradients as steep as 1 in 66 to contend with!

Once the train had passed I could not ignore the visual treat available at the turn of the camera.

Opposite:
'Warrior' scurrying across the embankment above Longwood Creek.

Veering away from the river the railway line emerges from Long Wood to cross Greenway Viaduct. This is Agatha Christie country, for the famous crime writer lived in Greenway House on the estate that is out of shot to the right.

Opposite:
The lower reaches of the estuary as seen from the estate. You don't need the detective skills of Monsieur Poirot to understand why the novelist settled here.

Having crossed the viaduct and passed through Greenway Tunnel the train approaches Churston.

Owing to space limitations at the termini, Churston became the engineering centre of the line.
The locomotive workshop on the right was built in 1991.

In this view north from the adjacent road bridge, the railway's
turntable is just visible behind the bushes on the right.

The train coasts down the gradient between Churston and Goodrington.

With a toot of the whistle No.4555 'Warrior' announces its imminent arrival at Goodrington Sands.

Opposite:
On the southbound route passengers are treated to the scenic joys of a sea
view that covers a wide expanse of Torbay.

The day-trippers returning from Dartmouth will soon be joined by the red-faced beachcombers and sun worshippers that have spent the day by the sea at Goodrington. Paignton and journey's end is but a few minutes away.